TURTLE

LIFE CYCLES

Words that look like **this** can be found in the glossary on page 24.

BookLife PUBLISHING

©2018
BookLife Publishing
King's Lynn
Norfolk PE30 4LS

Printed in Malaysia.

A catalogue record for this book is available from the British Library.

ISBN: 978-1-78637-379-3

Written by:
Madeline Tyler

Edited by:
Kirsty Holmes

Designed by:
Danielle Rippengill

LIFE CYCLES

CONTENTS

WHAT IS A LIFE CYCLE?

All animals, plants and humans go through different stages of their life as they grow and change. This is called a life cycle.

Human Life Cycle

Baby

Child

Adult

WHAT IS A TURTLE?

A turtle, or sea turtle, is a type of **reptile**. Turtles have hard shells on their backs and **flippers** that help them swim.

EGGS

Female turtles lay eggs with soft shells. Turtle eggs are white and round and look a bit like golf balls.

A collection of turtle eggs in a nest is called a clutch.

Turtles lay around 110 eggs in a nest. Some turtles lay up to eight clutches every nesting **season**.

Turtle eggs have to be hidden from predators because turtle mothers return to sea after laying them.

Female turtles dig a hole on the beach to lay their eggs into. They cover the eggs with sand to keep them safe and warm.

A warmer nest produces more female turtles and a cooler nest produces more male turtles.

HATCHLINGS

Baby turtles are called hatchlings. Hatchlings break out of their egg using a special tooth called a caruncle. The hatchlings work together to dig out of the nest.

Hatchlings stay in their eggs for 45 to 70 days.

When they reach the surface, hatchlings head towards the sea. They must be fast so that they are not eaten by predators.

The hatchlings swim far out to sea. The next years are sometimes called the 'lost years'. During this time, the hatchlings become **juveniles**.

No one is sure exactly where the turtles go or what they get up to during the 'lost years'.

Scutes are like armour plates that protect the turtle!

Turtles also shed their skin.

When turtles grow and become juveniles and adults, they shed the scutes on their shell. This keeps their shell healthy and means that new, bigger scutes can grow.

TURTLES

Turtles become adults when they are almost fully grown. Turtles do most of their growing when they are juveniles, and do not grow much more when they are adults.

Female turtles must find a **mate** so they can lay eggs. They return to the beach they hatched on to lay their eggs.

TYPES OF TURTLES

There are seven different types of sea turtle. Green turtles are the only **species** of sea turtles that are **herbivores**. Green turtles eat lots of seaweed.

They are called green turtles because of their greenish skin.

Leatherback turtles are the largest type of sea turtle. They are black and have long, soft shells. They mostly eat jellyfish.

TURTLE TRIVIA

Turtles can hold their breath underwater for around seven hours. Some turtles **hibernate** underwater for several months.

Turtles are coldblooded. This means that they must **bask** in the sun to warm their blood and their bodies.

WORLD RECORD BREAKERS

World's Largest Nesting Group

The largest group of nesting leatherback turtles was found in Gabon, West Africa. Between 15,730 and 41,373 female turtles all used these beaches to lay their eggs.

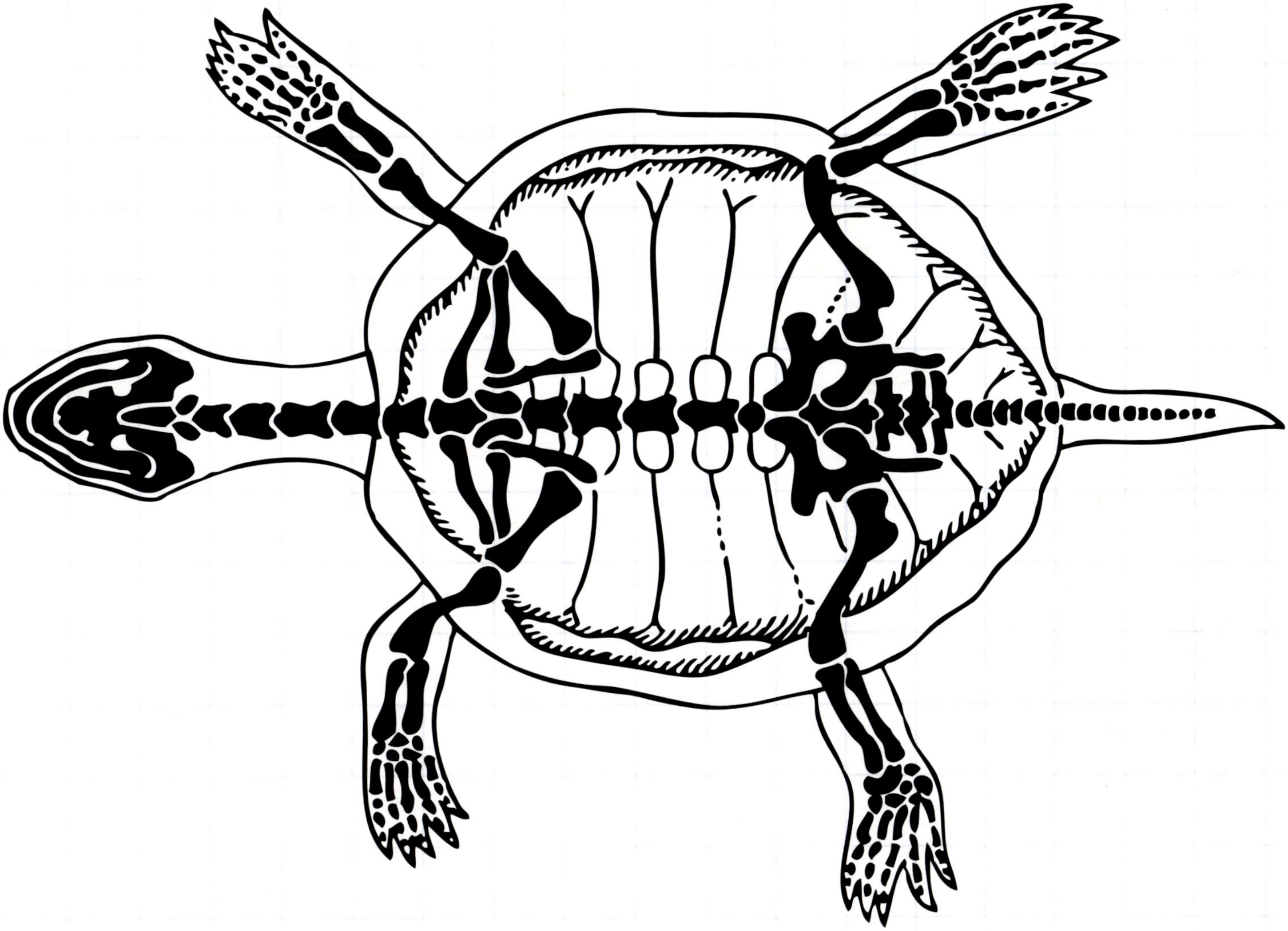

World's Oldest Turtle Fossil

The world's oldest sea turtle fossil was found in Colombia. It is around 120 million years old!

LIFE CYCLE OF A TURTLE

1

A female turtle lays a clutch of eggs into a nest in the sand.

2

Hatchlings break free using their caruncle.

3

The hatchlings swim out to sea where they grow into juveniles.

4

When the turtles are old enough to mate, they return to the beach to lay their eggs.

GET EXPLORING!

What else can you learn about sea turtles? Maybe you could visit an **aquarium** and see a turtle for yourself?

GLOSSARY

aquarium a place containing tanks of many different sea creatures

bask to lie in a warm, calm place, usually in the sun

flippers wide, flat limbs (on turtles, whales, or other animals) used for swimming

herbivores animals that only eat plants

hibernate spend the winter sleeping, or in a dormant state

juveniles young and not grown-up yet

mate a partner (of the same species) who an animal chooses to produce young with

predators animals that hunt other animals for food

reptile a cold-blooded animal with scales

season a certain part of the year when a particular activity takes place

species a group of very similar animals or plants that are capable of producing young together

INDEX

PHOTO CREDITS

All images are courtesy of Shutterstock.com, unless otherwise specified. With thanks to Getty Images, Thinkstock Photo and iStockphoto. Frontcover – Rich Carey. 1 – Rich Carey. 2 – Jamie David Simpson. 3 – Sukpaiboonwat, hrui, Rich Carey. 4 – Pepsco Studio, Rawpixel.com, Odua Images. 5 – Davdeka. 6 – Muzairi Mustapa. 7 – Kalaeva. 8 – David Evison. 9 – apiguide. 10 – Volodymyr Burdiak. 11 – FamVeld. 12 – Allison Herreid. 13 – Rich Carey. 14 – Maciej Czekajewski. 15 – Maciej Czekajewski. 16 – Jamie David Simpson. 17 – ACEgan. 18 – Patryk Kosmider. 19 – StacieStauffSmith Photos. 20 – Maquiladora. 21 – Dn Br. 22 – antpkr, Heiko Kiera, orlandin, Andamansky. 23 – Rainer Plendl.